FULL MOON

MOON

Elin 156

Impressum

Bibliografische Information der Deutschen
Nationalbibliothek: Die Deutsche Nationalbibliothek
verzeichnet diese Publikation in der Deutschen
Nationalbibliografie; detaillierte bibliografische Daten
sind im Internet über dnb.dnb.de abrufbar.

© 2021 Elin 156
Herstellung und Verlag: BoD – Books on Demand,
Norderstedt
ISBN: 978-3-7526-6264-1

contents

1 *waxing crescent*

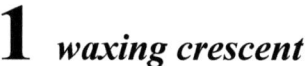

counterfeit love

do you remember the days
we spent outside on the meadow
covered with flowers?
where we forgot our sorrows
because we were talking
and laughing for hours?

take me back

does any kind of love have something like
an end or a beginning? I can only find my-
self in the middle of it, heavily spinning

I think I can hear what you're thinking and
you're not thinking out loud

soulmate

I would have lied for you, even if that meant
lying to myself

ripping out pages from my love letter
you never righted your wrongs
how foolishly I was hoping for the better
ripping you out from my thought process
thinking of you isn't clever
yeah, even though I promised to stay
you showed me
we weren't meant to last forever

I'm not good at
hiding or keeping my secrets
but you're the greatest secret
I have ever kept
you n I are like a blossoming flower
that I want to protect
and about the bond we have
I simply don't want to brag
it is something only between the two of us
something dearly bought
that I need to hold back

the abandoned home

the frames on the desk are rusty,
on the floor lies broken glass,
the shards became dusty,
and my heart's racin' fast

I vaguely remember the words
we threw across the room,
and when we said it's over,
and I silently hoped
you'd come back soon

the colours we painted on these walls
are slowly fading,
in the place
I am now standing,
in the place
we used to call home

my life is dark,
this room is dark,
who will take the paint brush,
and repaint these walls?

please say you're here, too,
I can't fix this on my own,
this place,
this messed-up relationship,
this abandoned home

I did not ask you to be my sun
that brightens up my whole life
or to be my moon
that shines on my darkest night
to beautify my sky for a brief moment
– maybe after the sunrise –
would've been enough
or am I still asking too much?

with you time froze
days were overly long,
even the sun didn't seem
to want to set
when we watched her
and played our favourite song

why did you leave?

I leafed through the book of our story and
saw we didn't have a happy ending

my eyes
saw
your eyes
revealing
all your lies
and I still decided
to forgive you

you take me up so high
I believe there is no ceiling
and only sky

I thought I knew you inside out
and all your secrets by heart
but I see, it wasn't the real you
it was only in my mind
and a kind of beautiful mirage

I talked about you
to my heart last night,
it repeated
you should be leaving,
I asked
why,
since it was still beating,
it replied
you have never noticed
how I was always bleeding,
for new air I was pleading
when I said
you deserve better,
please leave him

I promised
not to break the rule,
not to cry over you
yet I'm standing here
with my drink in my hand
still wondering
why this was the end

we just don't go together anymore
I wanted down to earth
whereas you wanted the whole damn sky

you said
you would
never let me
go
and I told you
some things
I never told
anyone else
before

we danced
under the stars,
watched the sun
rise and
set,
we really
went this far
just to
part with
*I wish we had never
met*

honestly, I'll never find someone like you,
someone that makes me feel the same way
you made me do

I can still
sense
the butterflies
in my stomach
that you gave me
when you
painted my mind
with all your
beautiful lies

I can hear you calling my name.
I feel like standing in the ocean while you're
somewhere in the hills, far away, for me not
reachable.
I tried to stay with you, move with you, to
keep my life aligned to yours, but all you did
was to distance yourself further, and perhaps
holding on to you was the mistake.

my thoughts revolve around you
like planets revolve around the sun

thought this would last forever
but I guess your idea of forever
was different from mine

I gave you love
you gave me nothing
you didn't change it
you didn't do anything
until I took my love away from you
forever

it's too late

even the loudest and the most crowded
places are quite and empty without you

without you

in the end,
you were nothing more than a bad decision

how come
we can't get this pride out of our way?
you don't text me, I don't text you
is this how relationships end these days?

will you
text back
when
I drunk text you
in the middle
of the night?
or will you
ignore it
so I regret it
when I wake up
in the morning?

relapse

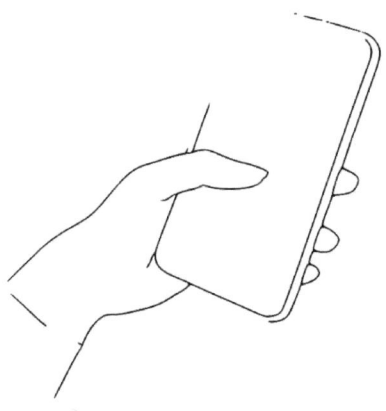

maybe it was my fault
my fault because I thought
this could be something special
something real

after all these days
it is still us that I chase
hoping what we're going through
is only a phase

I don't need you
to complete me,
I'm already
whole on my own
but that doesn't mean
I don't want you to be around
It's just
that you
messed it up
and I couldn't even recognise
half of myself
when I was with you

how many times have I swallowed my pride
for you, have I forgiven you things you had
never apologised for?

when you left …
did you think about coming back?

I knew it was over when I was no longer
scared of losing you

you may be different
but I was never really into mainstream

I still have our things here, hidden in a dusty
box under my bed – old tapes and CDs with
songs we listened to, songs I can no longer
hear, want to forget.
photos that told more beautiful stories than
words ever could.
no, I shouldn't keep all this …
but it's the only place on earth where there is
a happy us, or an us at all.

we need to slow it down
and turn around
before we move too fast
and we both crash

it's not like falling but more like floating in
space
without any fear of running out of oxygen

we are like
two parallel lines
we're similar
and we took the same direction
but our paths
never really crossed
and they unfortunately
never will,
we're distant
and we're close
but never close enough
and we will probably
never get any closer

honey dripped from your lips
but you didn't taste as sweet as you made
yourself look, not even a bit

I say much
until I don't
my mouth big
but I know
when to keep quiet
yeah,
I can teach you a lot
but no,
I cannot teach you
how to love me right

you are the moon to my ocean
causing tidal waves inside of me

if you were water
you would be calm,
you would calm me down
with your voice,
with the rustle of your waves
you would not be too cold
and not too warm,
you would be pleasant,
you would not be too much
and not too little either,
you would be just enough
If you were water
you would be deep,
within you
there's an undiscovered depth,
no one noticed,
and that's because
they can't swim,
but I can,
and I guarantee,
I'm not afraid to drown

faded pictures of you and I on the wall, on
the floor, it's like they are talking to me,
holding on to me, drowning me in an ocean
of memories, but I refuse to drown. I'll force
myself to dive back, come back to a reality
in which I must understand
that there is no more an us and you're in
these pictures but not here with me for a
reason.

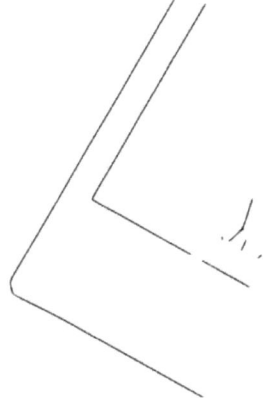

you are the lightning to my thunder
we are a perfect match
but together we cause danger and disaster

tell me lies
about you and I
tell me lies
the ones
that keep me
safe at night
tell me lies
yeah,
every time
a truth hurts inside

call me when you're in need,
when everything seems dark
and you can find no sleep
call me when it's cold,
when you can't find the road,
the road that leads you back home
call me when you're done,
done with everything and everyone
call me when they're gone,
and you're again feeling alone

call me, and I'll be there

like in *drugs you should try it*
I am glad that I found you on my way
after being down and lost for too many days

since the perfect versions
of you and I
only exist in my mind
reality must be wrong,
I have been living
in a dream, an illusion
for quite too long

when I said
I wanted to
go away with you
I didn't talk about
sitting in a car
or a plane
but in a space coupe
flying us to the moon

out in space

you tore down the ceiling, broke the
pictures, and the windows. I'm surrounded
by shards, debris and ashes. I should have
found another home a long time ago,
but this is our home and I'm still catching
myself in trying to find comfort in it.

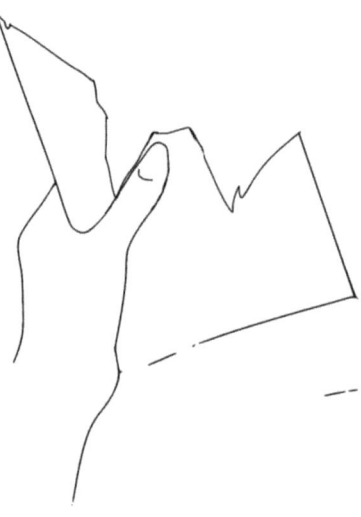

even if you should lose sight of each other
the universe will ensure you meet again – no
matter what forces try to separate you

soulmate

you told me
I have
become quiet
and a little bit
distant,
the truth is
I always
said enough,
you just
had to listen

can you imagine
that you were my everything
but at the same time
nothing at all?
you gave me so much
but took a lot more
away from me
you were
both the cure
and the poison,
both my angel
and my demon,
someone
I should let go of
but cannot forget

can you imagine?

in your hands
I placed my heart,
it was a soft and
a fragile part -
and you told me
at the very start
you'd not tear
my heart apart

broken promises

don't say it's complicated
or that we've become distant
when I'm one call away
one text message away
but I guess it's hard to convince someone
who does not want to stay

there is so much on my mind
so much in my heart that I want to share
with you
but you're not here anymore
you're nowhere to be found

you claim you wear loyalty inside of you
but is it unconditional and unlimited or will
you switch sides when you find someone
new?

in the present
- it seems like -
we're not meant to be
but maybe
when the sky is clear
and
when all the dark clouds
have disappeared
we'll see each other again

FULL MOON

I miss you
I sighed

you seemed confused
but I'm here

no,
I mean the old you

how did you see the pain
that was growing inside
or the thoughts
that were spinning in my mind
how did you see
that every word I was spitting
was a lie
as if your mind
could easily read mine

???

FULL MOON

I won't admit it was wrong
but I'm lowkey paying for every red flag
I was ignoring back then

FULL MOON

hiraeth,
I'm
homesick
for you
but
I will not
return to
you,
never again

the sun is
in my eyes,
it's cold,
golden leaves
are twirling
and dancing
on the ground,
I'm only here
because I promised myself
to wait on you,
maybe when you're back
you'll find me here again,
maybe I will be gone after some time
and you'll find here somebody else instead,
and only maybe
I will never see the wonder
I have then left on your face

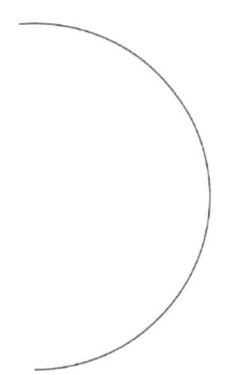

2 *first quarter*

you think too much,
yeah, I know

ephemeral, nothing lasts forever, not the sky,
not even you and I

FULL MOON

my world is ungraspable
I don't know where to begin
hopefully I'll find a place
where all my pieces perfectly fit in

I often find myself torn between
what I want and what I need
I guess my heart does not always want what
is good for me

I haven't changed, I'm just showing you a
side of me you have never seen before

part of me wants to be understood, another
part wants to leave you confused

do good things really take time or am I just a
fool with too much patience, and a heart
filled with a lie?

my thoughts protect me on some days and
destroy my most vulnerable parts on others

you're not
attached to me
but to the person
I was before
you keep on
searching for her
inside of me
but she's nowhere
to be found

I'm a lover and a hater, someone who holds
you close and pushes you away later

eye can see a lot
still eye am blind
as eye am not able
to fully open my mind

I have many wrongs beside my rights
and I hope God forgives me
for every tear you shed because of me
on your sleepless nights

you know it is a mistake
a bad decision that will cause a heart to
break
you are going to hurt someone
and you won't even feel bad,
you just know it is something you want and
you have to make

as
day and night
my soul
switches
from
light to dark
it has parts
you would love,
and parts
you would not
want
to know about

you should let me go, I'm bad for thee

sometimes I look at the starry sky and let it
remind me how small and temporary my
problems are

unexpected,
that's how
I left,
unexpected,
that's how
I came back

forever,
if a year has 525 600 minutes
how many minutes does forever have?
if a year has 365 days
how many days does forever have?
millions? billions? trillions?
who am I in this endless ocean
called forever,
and how big is the part
I am playing in it?

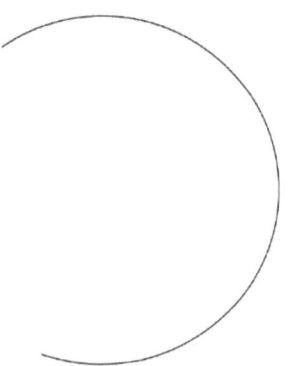

3 *waxing gibbous*

not full yet
but we're aiming for a change

change your mind, change your life
change yourself, change your world

a past
that always returns
is a past
you tried to drown,
is a past
you refused to face

if the loss brings you peace
it isn't a loss

trust me

don't take it personal
if I cannot reply now
I'm searching
for a little peace of mind

and it's going to take some time

someone's somewhere

someone's somewhere watching
your tears are counted
they will get what they deserve
and so will you

change takes courage, patience and a whole
lot of strength

life gives and life takes, and I am grateful
for this kind of balance

take me to
where my inner voice
is drowned out by the sound of the sea,
where my thoughts have no choice
but to leave my body
where the deep blue of the sea
covers the dark inside of me,
where my inner self can enfold
and the sun covers everything in gold

don't take me away until I am moved
and my soul is completely renewed

I wish I could just pluck you
yeah, pluck you out of my brain
like the hair I pluck
to bring my eyebrows in shape

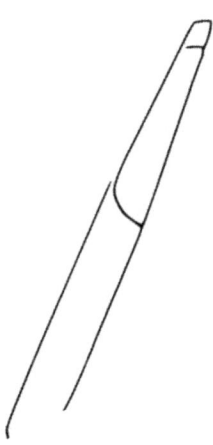

just as the wind carries away the leaves
life will carry away all your hardship
bringing you hope and some ease

don't lose this pureness of your heart
it's purer than any water I have ever seen

you must be willing to see
the beauty of the rain
before you impatiently wait
for the sun to rise again

you deserve to be more than just
somebody's *maybe*

you paid a lot
just to get a bit of their love
but will you believe me
when I say real love is for free
and don't cost a thing?

perhaps healing does not mean building an
entire house from the ruins but grabbing and
throwing away the stones you thought you
would never get rid of

step by step

don't judge
some of us experience things
you would not even want to
experience in your worst dreams

you caused
somebody else's
scars
only because
you couldn't handle
your own, and
that's not
how healing
supposed to work

your time is too precious to spend it waiting
on someone who does not value it

sometimes I want to be alone, sometimes I don't, you said.
you never really wanted to be left all alone, I assumed, you just wanted to be around someone who never puts your heart and your mind in two different places.

in life you will face many options, running
back to the one who hurt you shouldn't be
one

if you stay
things still won't change
they will remain the same
and only feed your pain

your heartbreak is
like the seasons
and
seasons end
seasons change
I can't promise you
sunshine and warmth
on december eight
or a longer lasting summer
with a winter arriving late
what I can say is
fallen leaves will be gone
blown away
water that was once frozen
will flow again
and

a heart that was
once broken

will love again

I wish I could take away your pain by just
smiling at you

walking away from you wasn't weak or
selfish, it was an act of self-love

I remember
when I told you
you are beautiful
as a rose
still I don't like
comparing you
to one
for roses die   when you
break
them
but
you,
yeah, you survived
and
wanted to be alive -
after
all
the
things
you have been through

love doesn't need any directions
if something is meant for you
it will naturally find its way to you

don't force it

self-harm
isn't always
cutting,
scratching
and injuring
your body,
it's also
your inner voice
criticising
and blaming you,
telling you
your worthless,
soaking up
every peaceful thought
in your head,
turning your
colourful mind
into a dark place,
and love
into hatred

be aware of both

you deserve a love that is not conditional, a
love that keeps you warm even on colder
days

do not confuse unconditionally loving them
with accepting their toxic behaviour, loving
someone's flaws is one thing but letting
someone mistreat you constantly has nothing
to do with love

you are somebody else's toxic

you're talking about how their toxic traits
lead to the breaking but how about your
toxic traits?

it's not always them

I love
when someone
opens up
about their
feelings and
their vulnerability,
imagine someone
being brave enough
to reveal
their true colours
in front of
a world that
always tries
to appear strong
and happy
when it's clearly
not the case

aren't you tired of the pretending?

hey, I've written so many letters to you but
you never wrote me back, you don't read
them, do you?? I'm still sorry for the things
I have done to you, but I never thought you
would kill us and throw us away...
I'm sorry, but yo-

* throws letter away *

me to me: he's not sorry

manipulator

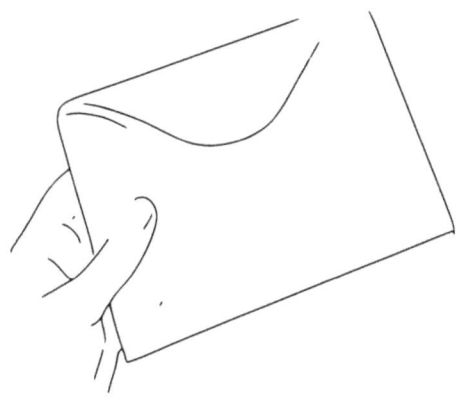

healing means finding yourself again, recognizing features from you from the past, right before everything was in the ruins

FULL MOON

I want you to fill others with a love
bright as the sun
just like her
you can fill greyish clouds
with your golden rays of light

the one who split you open won't be the one
who will sew you up again

read that again

I don't know
who told you to
hide that pain
yeah,
even if you should
decide to climb
to the top
of a mountain
to scream your lungs out
you are allowed
to do so

you are allowed
to show emotions
you are allowed
to show pain

you are soft
you feel
with your heart,
you think
with your heart
everything you say
comes
from your heart
and no,
you never asked
for being this soft
but baby,
that's you
and
that's what
makes you beautiful

you looked away and I started to cry
I desperately tried to make my eyes dry
but you took my hands,
both of 'em
and you showed me
that you understand,
you showed me
it is okay to cry

you are
the good
in your
side of the story
but what if
you are
the bad
in their
side of the story?

seriously,
it's not always them

it will ache
maybe for
some days,
a couple of months,
a year?
thoughts,
emotions,
inner voices
will haunt you,
you don't
understand it,
what is it that I hear?
the pain is
too much to carry,
you can't help
but to cry,
lose heavy tears,
but I'm here to tell you
to dry your eyes,
to see things more clear,
you need to
realise
that those thoughts,
the voices
are not really real

every step seems harder to me, as does
breathing, I have come a long way - I tell
myself - but when I turn around I see that I
have barely made any progress, I tell lies,
more and more lies to myself, to keep my-
self going, to keep myself doing what I have
been doing all along: slowly moving into the
hands of something that is obviously not
meant for me

you listen to the rain, to the raindrops hitting
the windowsill
as if they could take away your pain
you did this often, but this time it is not the
same
you're not crying anymore, though you're
tired, disappointed, and lying on the cold
hard floor
you continued listening to the sound
but promised to get over it
when there is silence, and the last drop hit
the ground

I choose to heal

the hair on
your face,
your arms,
your legs
don't make
you less
of a woman

social media
is giving you
an audience
and a voice
you'd not
have in real life
don't use it
to tell other woman
how they should dress,
or to leave a toxic comment
about how they are
(in your eyes)
wearing too less

healing from social media

true love will find you when you are least
prepared for it, and when it finds you
it will not leave you

if they cannot give you the love you give
don't waste your love on them

you're not waiting but they are letting you
wait, know the difference

I hope you find here the kind of comfort you
couldn't find anywhere else

to my dear reader

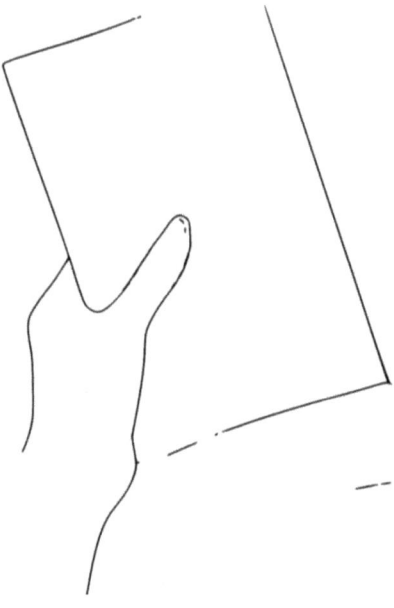

block them
while
they are
still typing
and go to sleep

it's over, honey

yes, you learn from mistakes, but I still wish
I had known better back then

to the person reading this: you're not here by chance, this is the sign you have been wait-ing for

let them go

the greatest gift you can receive is
someone's support, someone's love while
you're trying to heal from your wounds

there is beauty inside of you
a beauty you have not discovered yet

you are the artist of your life, draw it as you
like it and be as creative as possible

grounded by failure, courageous enough to
dream of the sky again

smiling to the songs you used to cry to is a
major progress, trust your healing process

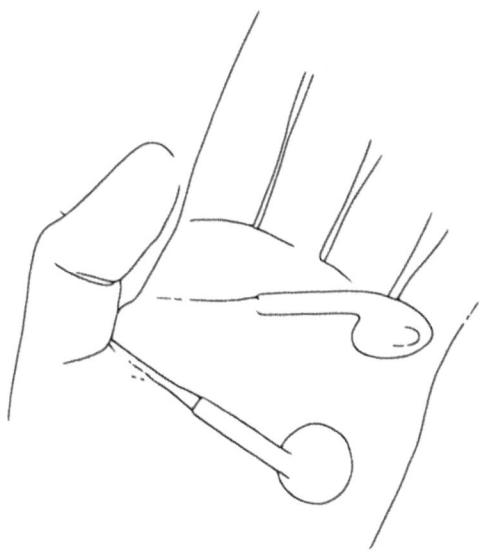

and when you start doubting yourself again
I will stand behind you and show you how
much I believe in you

all you need is
someone
who promises to stay
on your loneliest days
all you need is someone
who hugs you tight
on your rainiest days

your breaking is the key part of your
becoming

love your enemy

it was not you
who broke me
it was the self-doubt
and the anxiety
it was the bad thought
that kept me
awake at night
and the demons
that I still have to fight

my thoughts are the seeds of
my poetry, my flower
its roots will always remind me
of the pain I hid
its blossom
of what I have made of it

I don't know exactly
where the wind of fate is taking me
but I hope I will arrive safely
at the place that I need to be

never let your losses distract you from the
blessings you are constantly facing in your
life

in the end,
I don't own
anything
or anyone
in the end,
all I have
is myself,
and maybe
this is enough

remember:
you're not
just here
to get inspired
you are
here
to inspire

what to do when you're feeling down:

1. get out of your bed
2. take a shower (and if it helps: cry in the shower, let it out!)
3. look in the mirror and … smile (it helps!)
4. eat something!! cook your favourite food or order a pizza, don't forget to call your friend
5. buy the bag, the lipstick, the shoes you always had an eye on, treat yourself!
6. create a playlist of your favourite songs and share it with your friends
7. watch your favourite series
8. do something you always wanted to do: travel, go to a concert, write a book, learn an instrument (you're full of talent!)
9. spend time with yourself, get to know yourself better (your inner self wants to tell you something)

better days are near, stay patient

dear reader,

FULL MOON is divided into three different chapters, which I named after the phases of the moon (the phases before the full moon), these phases are at the same time an allusion to your development: everything you have experienced in your life made you the person you are today. but you have surely noticed that there is no chapter on the phase full moon (generally the other phases are missing), I have specifically left out this phase because I don't really think that a person will ever fell full or complete in their life time, we are constantly changing and that is what this book is meant to illustrate. but what you should hold on to is that even your worst days will make you grow and glow.

if you ever think you are standing in front of a wall again, then remember that this will only strengthen you and you will eventually be able to tear this wall down. you got this.

yours truly,
elin

I wanted to do an *about the author* but I'm just a normal girl, you get 10 facts instead:

1. I was born on June 15, 2000
2. I live in Germany
3. I love travelling and discovering new places
4. I love music (especially r&b / hip hop music, always hit me up if you're looking for new songs)
5. I'm a student teacher
6. 5 is my lucky number
7. changes do not scare me
8. I'm an introvert
9. I'm a workaholic
10. and oh yeah, my name is Elin